Before Kodachrome

■ ■ ■

Don Schofield

FutureCycle Press
Mineral Bluff, Georgia

Copyright © 2012 Don Schofield
All Rights Reserved

Published by FutureCycle Press
Mineral Bluff, Georgia, USA

ISBN 978-1-938853-01-2

For Litsa and my parents, all of them.

Contents

■■ I 9
The Immortals 11
Chosen 12
First Journey, Alone 14
Driving Thessaly 16
A Child's 99 18

■■ II 21
Before Kodachrome 23
2619 Van Ness Blvd 24
Keeping the Monsters Moving 25
Dutch Clock 27
Devotion 29
Divorce 32
After the Divorce 34
Rummaging 35
New Parents 37

■■ III 41
Ars Poetica 43
That Blur 45
The Trouble with Gender 47
About the Bears 49
Constellations 51

■■ IV 57
Demolition 59
Adolescence 61
Good Posture 64
Maybe, CA 66

Acknowledgments 71

The way up is the way back.
       —*Heraclitus*

I

The Immortals

> *Hera is not...mother as mother but mother as wife.*
> —The Gods of Greece

Mother writes that she can't control her bowels.
Pain runs up her spine, down her arms.
Her husband, who left her, comes 'round every Sunday
for a meal. Of Reno, the nights alive
with neon, bells, whoops of truckers
at blackjack and keno, she won't write.
She married my father, stayed till he beat her,
then longer for the courage to be lonely again.

I call them immortal, him standing over her,
fire in his eyes, her running off
with the next man who took her to his bed,

because, as we know, even gods
are human—vain, contentious, disorderly
in their wants. Only death is eliminated.
And the need to believe in an ideal world.

Chosen

Best to think of my father as Abraham
raising his knife, a red-haired
angel there to take me to heaven—
how else explain betrayal,
the end of certainty? I was four,

in a Fresno bar, turning slowly
on a barstool, waiting as he talked
to a red-haired woman, the late
noon sun pressing through blackened
windows. He brought me there
because he brought me everywhere—
on the Greyhounds he drove, to hotels,
restaurants, card rooms—
the son he chose, the one he took
when he left my mother and brother behind,

and I was glad to go, dizzy with joy
when he carried me on his shoulders out the door—
after so many months I was still
pretending sleep when he came to bed
at first light: finally, what I craved,
the weight of his exhausted body on the mattress,
stale smell of whiskey and Old Spice,
his great snoring. Around noon

we'd both awake. He'd comb my hair,
unfold the *Daily Double* over lunch.
You're my buddy, he'd declare
as we walked to post office, laundry
or bank. He'd sway me on his knee when I cried,
like Mom. *Why me,* I wanted to ask,
and not my brother? but never did

because that day, in that bar, he suddenly turned,
asked if I wanted to live with this woman
here in Fresno. I stared at that stranger,
her thick make up, low-cut
blouse—this an angel?—
then back at him, eyes pleading
for me to go. I remember

grabbing his neck and whispering (though I meant
to scream), *No, I won't go, you chose
me*, arms pushing me away,
face sliding into irretrievable
darkness; remember

agreeing somehow,
that woman's hand gripping mine
as we stepped into the Fresno sun,
cars ablaze with the flame
burning in my red eyes—
so this was Paradise.

But mostly I think of him
alone in that bar, no god
having intervened. What was left
but to set his glass down
like a bleeding knife, rise
in his ashen uniform
and go to work.

First Journey, Alone

For an hour and twenty minutes
he's been watching a couple
lifting and setting down a suitcase,
two sailors flirting with passersby,
a woman with crying baby in one arm,
daughter with half-eaten sandwich
in the other. For a moment he thought
how they're family, all in this
together. Then indifference set in.
He's nothing to them and they're nothing
to him, just faces sliding
across glass when the big doors open.

The whole depot slides with them—
tall racks of magazines
in the gift shop, dusty shelves
of model Greyhounds and dolls
with outstretched arms,
bright pinball machines, a spinning wheel
that tells fortunes and stamps pennies
with The Lord's Prayer, even the drivers
in the diner's corner booth, their hushed talk
of a Porsche that hit the Tahoe Express
head-on—all dissolves
when the dispatcher announces from the rafters
San this, *El* that.

↓

He steps up into the cool dark
of a Scenicruiser, finds a seat
in the back, watches the last passengers board.
When a stranger sits beside him,

squeezes his arm and asks his name,
the boy looks down
at workers tossing luggage like lost souls
into the Greyhound's underbelly. Leaving the city,

it's the symmetry of orchards he glares at,
smudge pot flames dancing on the cool
tinted glass. Rows of oil rigs
pump out the slowly
descending night—and now this man's
pressing his thigh,
asking where he's from,
where he's headed.

↓

The dead were laid out
along the side of the road
in drifts of snow—he saw them
as the drivers kept telling and retelling
their story. Indifference wavered
as he placed a napkin over his fork and spoon,
stroked the bodies lying there,
imagined the bus he's now on
plummeting the full length of a slope,
passengers falling into each other's arms—

But this is *his* story,
so the boy, alone,
clings to a fistful of stamped pennies
and never forgives those who trespass against him.

Driving Thessaly

> *A bump in the road. Hell, a nice shape, but it reminds you*
> *of your father, where he's buried.*
> —Andrew Wyeth

South of Larissa
the roads are too narrow
to go fast, too many tractors
along the shoulder, too many roadside
fruit stands. This highway's so straight, so endless,
it could be Hwy 99
north of Fresno, each bump
that one bulge in an otherwise
flat route through orchards and towns, the place
I imagined as a boy they'd bury my father.

He botched that death.
Instead curled up and let the strokes come
one by one, let his hands dangle from the bed
like rotting pears. I wrote of his dying, again and again,
how I could touch the full length of his absence,
feel his pulse fading

for years. Now I drive to understand
why the light here is the light of the San Joaquin
in my childhood, why walnut trees here too
are painted white, why men climb thin ladders
to throttle the branches and walnuts fall
like tears. I know I've botched love,
wanting something more from words,
forgetting that *art only goes as far*

as love goes, so at every
washed-out muddy place I'd be up to my elbows

trying to make him anew—roots for ears,
sticks for arms, shattered glass for eyes
and teeth. I'd want to leave him
in wind, rain and the splash of passing traffic
to die another slow death…but, no,

I'd lick him smooth like a stray dog
licks the placenta from pups born dead,
thrums dirt with her paws to cover them up,
resignation and terror in her eyes
as she limps off to find some food.

And all repeats, mile after mile,
towns and orchards, orchards and towns,
that dog, I imagine, pausing at a fruit stand
to sniff an empty chair,
her tail vaguely wagging—is that
joy?—bump-bump
as love moves on.

A Child's 99

What if you took the wrong bus,
wound up headed for Portland or Elko—
would the same howling semis pass,
same billboards for Gillette and Oldsmobile?
Would you slide to that same cone of light,
rest your head on that same smudge
of hair oil? When the bus pulls in
to another depot little more
than a gas station, dusty elms
propping up the failing light—
same baggage tossed and shoved?
same passengers boarding or getting off?
same out-of-state plates you count
no matter what state you're in?

Wherever you stop for supper
there'll be fumes hovering over the diner
and, inside, loud voices, clatter of plates
and glasses. Better out back
in the empty lot that's always there,
kicking dirt clods with your heel. Who cares
if your shoes get grimy, if you eat
or not, if you step inside an abandoned
horse trailer, breathe in the wafts
of urine and hay. Gazing through the jagged hole
where the window was, you'll imagine
the weight of hooves striking
fresh shit; bright star on your forehead,
you'll glide through the night,
your own constellation—Appaloosa—
in a firmament of moonlit factories,
blinking radio towers, oil derricks
decked with lights. Fixed in that sky,

you won't be a smudge of doubt
riding dark orchards and fields,
town to town, depot to depot,
won't need to listen for that wine bottle
someone always kicks as he leaves,
its bouncing strut to strut down the long
row of seats your own
impatient stomping, its sound
as it falls from the last step—your hoof
hitting asphalt.

II

Before Kodachrome

I love this snapshot of the boy
posing in his Sunday best—white

trousers, sweater, even his hair
seems white. He's looking down

at the lawn deep in shadow, smiling
in light so bright it almost

washes him out.
And this one of his room:

Davey Crockett curtains,
Superman bedspread, Apache war bonnet

on the wall. A patch of light
is spreading over his face and arms;

ample darkness, though,
behind the door,

under the bed, surrounding
legs and feet. In that dreamy silence

before the others woke,
he's caught between two oblivions,

looking up from his bed, smiling,
in light so bright he's almost

not there.

2619 Van Ness Blvd

Even then, 1957,
that house was crumbling,
plaster falling from its ceiling
like pages from a book. Yet here,

in this photo on the front lawn, it's Sunday,
I'm eight years old forever,
arms around that mother
hard and straight as a door.
House, was it you I loved?

If I could know just half your thoughts,
feel your long-gone warmth
like the ivy climbing your walls…
House that towers in memory, strong
and beautiful, you who saw us fall
from love, that world come unhinged, tell me,

was it her despair or yours,
the swamp-cooler's mournful drone?
the cuckoo's insistent, oracular song?
the brooding of ballerinas
on her disheveled dresser

as all along your papered walls
that horse and carriage raced headlong
into a darkening forest? —Oh, House,
hold on, so I can,

to Sunday, to love, to 1957,
that bright grey lawn.

Keeping the Monsters Moving

Above our garage a rooster,
a black squeaky weather vane,
would point each day to where that father
had gone in his old spattered Cadillac
to paint houses, tar roofs.

He came back one night with Dan,
a hired hand: quiet, well-mannered
but sneaky about his drinking. Sanding the dresser,
he did the Mash, he did the Monster
Mash. Hip cocked, feet shuffling,
sweat running down his dust-
caked cheeks, he did the dance
that got the monsters moving,

singing the words out loud
as if he hadn't heard me come from school
with my bag of plastic army men,
spread the twirling bazookas,
the marksmen dancing with jeeps
over drums of pitch, piled tarps,
the wobbly workbench with stacked brushes,
cans of putty and Dutch Boy paints.

He left one night on a drunk
and that father came back with Wheelin'
& Dealin' Bob, bottle in his pocket,
singing *John McGrew was a fucking fool,
fucked all the teachers on the first day of school....*
A joke at first, his laughter
filling the garage, but soon a dull
repetition, a vulgar reminder
to stay away.

Still, that word had power.
He kept trying to get me to say it.
I remember finally standing
on a pile of tarps,
lip stuck on the first consonant,
feeling like the Dutch Boy
atop his ladder, that bright word
in the swath of my paintbrush, and even more
like the overalls dangling from a nail—
flayed skin of a beast
still roaming the dark garage—

f…f-f, I stuttered,
Bob laughing, coaxing me on,
me and my army guys in a stream of light,
black rooster squeaking, turning
toward impending weather.

Dutch Clock

Shades drawn. The living room
dark at noon. On the mantle
Dutch children ride a totter.
The girl waves on tick. The boy
kicks on tock. You're on the couch
pretending to nap, wondering
why they're always happy. You're not

on nights that father's home.
You sit in your corner of the couch,
wait for the show to start:
first a *har-de-har-har* from The Honeymooners,
a *Shut up, Alice* from Ralph,
then that father plops down
into his armchair, beer in hand. That mother's up,
pointing as she stands over him.

When he grabs her arm,
she twists away. When he pushes her,
she falls to the couch, then rises, calling out
accusations. He stands,
shouting forbidden words as he turns
the volume up, her response so shrill
he's up against her, fist raised,
her arms crossed in defiance.

To the moon, Ralph shouts
to laughter and applause, and you know,
staring at those rosy-cheeked children, it's time
for her to fall to the carpet, crying, waving
for him to stop, go, leave her
alone. *How sweet it is,* Ralph calls
as you, smiling hard, slip into the dark.

When silence finally comes,
she's in their bedroom, he's on the couch,
and you're tossing and turning in your room,
those children rising and falling
from inside your dream. Sometimes rage
twists at your throat, and you kick and kick
as they wave from far away. Sometimes
you're trapped inside glass, invisible
but for the flickering blue light
you reflect, and all you hear
is mother-tick, father-tock.
Sometimes you fall so deep
into fear you can't rise,

but always, next morning, you're there
in the kitchen hutch. *Everything's fine,*
they insist with their stiff smiles,
and even the fridge hums
as she fries eggs and he sips
coffee and you butter your toast.
How sweet it is, you say,
your voice pitched too high for irony
or truth. So *har-de-har-har*
to the fridge, *Shut up, Alice*
to the dripping faucet, *To the moon*
to yourself as you leave for the living room

to hear what those kids might say
if at least they could speak the truth:
how this craving for departure
rises and falls, but never leaves;
how nothing matters after a while
but holding on; how we're all behind glass,
kicking and smiling, pulling the shade
as the sun rises.

Devotion

Monsignor asked my Cherokee
    father to paint an old
        chipped statue of the Virgin.

Summer nights
    he scraped and sanded and dipped
        his brush into leftover

house paint, gave her
    a cloak blue from the Tripp's
        house, sandals brown

as our fence, hands
    and cheeks the pink enamel
        of our bathroom.

            ↯

I remember the unveiling: Monsignor
    in gold embroidered vestments,
        tulle pinned to the girls'

hair, us boys,
    closest to her niche
        just beyond the railing,

fidgeting in our pews as we mumbled
    her endless litany—till one
        nudged the next and we all

started giggling
    at the hint of red on her lips,
        her palm raised to the vague

outline of a nipple. Monsignor
    halted Mass, came down,
        yanked the Virgin from her pedestal,

demanded my father
    leave with her
        that instant.

        ↙

For so long now
    I've wanted to fill that empty niche,
        that half-domed firmament

of gold-daubed stars
    and purple from our porch windows,
        with his image—

not the man who stole
    from houses he was painting, that gambler,
        carouser, drunk swaying

at his workbench past dawn,
    but he who carried me
        to the attic, set me on his knee,

told me stories of his statue
    covered with dust: how his people,
        driven across the Mississippi,

carried her into lands
    never heard of; how they rescued her
        from his grandparents' burning cabin,

passed her on, one aunt
    to the next, Oklahoma
        to California; how he

still believed in the Blessed Virgin,
    this Corn Goddess,
        this Clan Mother. His warm

whiskey breath in my ear,
    I could barely see
        his black, deep-set eyes,

his scraped knuckles and thick,
    scarred fingers
        stroking her cheek,

his cracked
    lips in purple shadows
        mumbling a chant for the world.

Divorce

Not her thick, dark hair in the mirror,
perfect arc of her breasts. Not lying close,
with long gazes, silly names
for each other. Not the small fine hairs on her chin....
Let those memories drift away like dust
the wind kicks up on this island
in the middle of the Aegean. Let that wind
wear me down to the one memory I need: you,
sad father I had for awhile, last seen
in that dingy I-80 motel,
sweating on crumpled sheets, head propped
on a stained pillow, rusty wheelchair in a corner,
nurse gone, toilet running (not from you,
you joked). You kept saying it was her fault
you drove your car into a telephone pole,
snapped your spine; kept wanting to know,
after so many years, where she was, who
she was with, kept crying and apologizing for your life
and mine. Or maybe I need a worse memory:

ten years earlier, when I was eleven,
a cab drove up. I heard it
from my room, looked out to see the cabby
lift you to the curb, then drive off.
You wheeled yourself to the front door
(how happy I was to see you there),
rang the bell, and started yelling: *Whore!*
Bitch, slut! Let me in!
I'm your husband! Words
I want to yell at my own wife,
who told me it's over. I must go. Your wife
told me to go back to my room,

covered her ears and called the police
while you kept rolling up and down the sidewalk.
I heard the thump-thump of rubber wheels,
saw light glancing off spokes, pale legs
when you threw your blanket to the grass,
tangled tubes, urine bag swaying
with each turn. When you came up
to the door again, banging your forehead
against the screen, I gazed in horror
at your bloodshot eyes, the numb pink
penis in your lap. The police arrived,
covered your legs, strapped arms and waist
to your chair, lifted you into the waiting pickup,
and still you were yelling as the truck pulled away—
You can't divorce me! I'll never
let you go!

    Here on this island I've come to,
thanks to you I don't yell those words—
I let the landscape say it all:
tall weeds with spiked heads
lean from the clefts of cooled volcanic rock
all the way down to the sea, its blue-green depths
inaccessible from here. On the horizon
a thick fog settles. Somewhere beyond
she's brushing her long black hair. A few strands
drift to the floor... —No,
not memories of her, but of you,
tragic father, showing me how far
not to go.

After the Divorce

she bought me a Raleigh,
the one I'd always wanted—

metal-flake green
with chrome-plated handlebars,

a generator whirring as the lamp
on the fork glowed. Together we'd pedal

through long shadows of pines
along the esplanade, tires hissing, asphalt

cooling, everyone out on their porches
or strolling Van Ness at dusk. I'd coast

ahead of her with a boy's impatience,
gears clicking, our dog snuffling

driveways, curbs, the wide,
precise California lawns.

Smooth hum of generator.
Steady flow of light

through gathering darkness. Easy
not to see dust swirling up

in the wake of passing cars,
not to feel, so light,

the weight of something lost
settle over our new freedom.

Rummaging

Opening the bureau drawer, I lean
into the dark waft of mildew,
pull out a snapshot: Fresno,
the boy kneeling in leaves
by the back stoop, hugging his dog,

a present it seems,
last birthday in that city—
dog that loved the love of others,
never growled, never bared her teeth,
quickly fell, spread her legs

to offer her vulnerable underside,
a fervent craving to surrender,
like leaves falling to the lawn
each autumn. I can't
remember that birthday,

this photo, that particular
corner of the yard: all that happened
before love was carted off,
a pile of leaves. Yet here they are:
boy, dog, a yard full of leaves

in this torn, cracked print I hold
gently, an object of affection;
affection, too, for the boy
kneeling there, fifty years,
smiling, waiting for what?

A cold weight curling up,
dropping back—I feel it
deep inside, then vague smoldering at a curb

in rain, then more rain
sweeps away the boy, his dog, that yard,

till the memory of Fresno
is a dark, cluttered river, deep flood
of the dead gnashing teeth
pale as those grapes that once hung
over the back fence,

juiceless grapes that never fell—
Drop the print,
the boy whispers, *let it fall*
back into the dark.
Fifty years.

New Parents

Fresno in August. Asphalt melting.
Heat waves rising. The swamp-
cooler dripping.

                Fat flies
thump the glass—out, get out
and then they want in.

From the living room dark
he stares out at wind clawing leaves
across the yard, into the street.

Suitcase packed with all he needs—
folded shorts, flowery shirt
and comic books—he's ready
to meet his new parents,

Mother Odd, Father Even,
smoke spewing from the depths of their foundry

like bricked-in Fresno.

                ↯

With coon claws and cheshire smiles
they'll stroke him to sleep,

then slice deep into his heart
worn down already, pound his dreams

like tattered flags, pound the red-
veined gall, pound and cut and pound
till they get to his birth-anger,

lay a wreath for that wrath.

Then they'll stitch him tight,
fix a sail over the arc of ribs,

a small raft of one boy,
face soft as hammered bronze.

↯

When he steps through the foundry doors,
let earth be hard, hands
firm.

  Mother Odd, Father Even,
you who make him new
again—

Let the world flow smoothly past.
Let dust bloom where he steps.
Let his comic book version of tomorrow

be pure as his flowery shirt, pure
as every second he stares out
at bright empty space, sure it all ends
with truth and justice.

    Don't tell him
at eight years old
he's leaving love behind.

↯

When the cab arrives,
bright yellow this time,

she'll come, walk him out, tears gleaming
on the soft edge of her cheek.

Never again love this large.

The gap-toothed driver
smiles, opens the door, his leather seat
scalding the boy's fist
as he turns, looks one last time:

pines along the esplanade,
wide lawn,
green porch,
her face

in shimmering waves of heat.
Pound him there.

III

Ars Poetica

(Thessaloniki, on turning 56)

What I want from a poem this far away
is to get back to the boy who kicked cones
and talked to trees and heard the bark
bark. Pleasure was his motive for rolling boulders,

and curiosity: what could live
under such weight?—
grubs pulling with their whole bodies to regain
the dark, and snakes, rattles upright, heads swaying....

I remember that father with pick and shovel
digging a trench down the slope, the six-foot
galvanized pipes swaying as he lowered them
into a groove of red earth.

He wrapped horsehair around the ends,
taped the joints, replaced the skin
of needles and moss, what remained
of lizard, pine and crow.

Soon faucets dripped a rhythm
I could count all night as deer gathered
in the orchard below, though nothing
stopped our neighbor's shotgun blast

echoing in a tangle of directions,
nor the knowledge that by morning,
hanging from his porch—
buck, fawn or doe. But why?

Because he hauls apples all the way to Mariposa?
Because he gives, now and then, a shank to us?

Because so many want his Golden Delicious,
deer must inevitably fall?

Drip, drip-drip....

Fifty years and two continents away.

That Blur

in the corner of this snapshot
    could be a pine cone
dropping into eddying shadows,

skippers floating, or a trout
    lipping the pool's surface. In this photo,
more dream than memory,

there's a sprawling oak
    cradling the moon in its branches,
thin light pouring

on mossy boulders, on roots
    in the muddy bank, on bones of birds
in dust the boy always trolls

for casings hunters drop. He blows
    the brassy edge of each one,
calling quail, owl and dove

as he wades the stream,
    then climbs a trunk fallen
from the opposite clearing.

Will I figure out that blur
    as he sits atop the naked heartwood,
feels the scent of mint and thyme,

the thin light itself
    washing through him,
or will waking again send that boy

fleeing down splintered paths
    where deer now come

to sniff the air,

and wolves, turning their heads,
    catch his scent?
Are wolves that shadowy blur, their quick,

easy gait that one
    last flicker
in the corner of this snapshot?—

that instant, that always
    receding moment when
he and place were one.

The Trouble with Gender

    for Harita

After a long evening of distinctions,
a man's nature, a woman's,
somewhere between dream and memory,

a face is sinking through pressing bodies, warm arms
like swaying reeds, rocks crumbling like days,
thousands of days, shifting layers of the life
a boy must grow into. Who can say

where his body will take him,
now ahead, now in retrograde.... For now
let it settle on solid ground—

the Sierras: soft blue of heaven
in the mountains above, red glint of boulders
in the canyon below,

waist-high to a hunting father
naming trees, stroking ferns, offering fists
of wild berries. The boy leans into the warm
calloused palm stroking his hair—

such strength, such male knowing.
When that man raises a heavy Winchester,
why dream on, so many quail

falling, deer stumbling, and who could fly
with boy-arms, only a heavy arc
crashing through branches? Why stare

transfixed by your own warm blood, sprung nape,
eyes glaring with pure terror, their blue-
grey glint same as the rifles
hanging on the cabin wall?

He touches triggers, smooth stocks,
sees the red glaze of his own
skinned body dangling from the porch.

Now he's the moosehead over the couch—
glass eyes, stiff fur, huge
spongy lips that will never speak

of her great torso now gone, that clearing
she stepped into. Morning,
dream shifting like sediment,
the boy rises into manhood,

body anchored, like it or not,
to that moose, her retrograde
hunger for berries,

someone to lick.

About the Bears

I'd climb the mountain paths near our cabin
afraid of bears, though I knew to run
downhill so their short front paws
would give way and they'd roll on past me,

knew a Blue Bear's more black
than blue, an Alaskan Bear's nine
feet "long," my books say, but I'd
say "tall,"

knew a Moon Bear full grown
is my height,

that after mating season
a male will wander off,
scrounge brush for a den
or burrow into a tree's roots,
sleep away his "winter lethargy."

↙

Maybe, lost in the woods, I stumbled upon this cabin.

Maybe Mama Bear took me in
to keep Papa Bear from wandering off.

Maybe the records she plays—
"All Shook Up," "The Great
Pretender"—tell the real story,
how she married a bear who scares her,
who hangs his kill on the wall
so she hangs Blue Boy in the bedroom.

All I know is that Papa is short and hairy,
rough-faced and ugly when he's drunk,

that when he yells at Mama
or swipes at her with his heavy paw,
I want to stand up to him, tall as Blue Boy,
fireplace, forest and mountains receding behind me—

but here I'm small and there's no downhill.

↓

The bruise on her cheek is darker
than Blue Boy, bluer than the bedspread
in a heavy tangle on the floor,
blue as the peacock feather on her dresser.

Asleep at last on the tall metal bed, she's beautiful,
blanket rising, almost trembling, as she breathes,
a peacock in the wild, the song of a peacock—
a loud, frightening screech,
my books say—deep inside her.

Now it's enough to know
my black eye makes me
a bear—a Blue Bear
rolled up in the bedspread
on the cold stone floor,
ready to sleep my winter lethargy away.

Constellations

The Dream

Swinging out on a tattered rope
over a still pool, kicking
toward Orion, Capricorn,
the Elliptical Equator,

toward Andromeda, Coffin Corner,
Water Jug, his rope knotted
to that oak at the center of the universe,
the boy turns, lets go,

plummets lightly, quietly,
arms wide to constellations
shimmering on the pool's surface. When he hits,
stars collide, sky shatters—

all the heavens sundered. You'd think
nothing could survive. But Orion
wobbles back into place
and the boy finds his own spot

in warm, feathery silt, where he'd stay
forever, if lungs like wings
didn't lift him toward Andromeda,
Coffin Corner, Water Jug.

The Journey

He wakes often in the back seat,
dust thick on the windows
through Coarsegold, Nippenowausee,
and here the cliff-face
so close he can almost read
its glyphs of lichen and moss, its message

gone in the next turn, car jostling,
wheels sliding—No,

not gone, just different:
now burnt pines
are ragged *As*, stumps are gaping
*O*s, tapping pistons ellipses
joining startled quail to squirrels
munching acorns to a doe
lifting her head in a clearing—
gone as the road rises,

drops into the next valley.
He knows this landscape,
each turn of phrase, knows,
sliding down in his seat,
eyes heavy again, he can never be
that stream lost in leaves,
those larches blooming in a doorless,
roofless cabin; at best that heifer

grazing like a good reader
on a world half-recalled, half-
made up, or the scarecrow
winking at the boy in the rear-
view mirror as the car climbs
toward the setting sun, switch-back
to switch-back, the two of them nodding,
Yes, Yes, as dust erases it all....

The Opening

Pushing open the heavy wooden door.
The smell of winter stale, pervasive.

Lighting lamps in the cold dark.
Building a fire.

Shining his flashlight under the bed,
behind the closet, up into

every dark corner of the rafters.
Finding in the backs of drawers

pungent rats' nests made from
mattress stuffing, shredded magazines.

Lowering with iron tongs
the block of ice—huge, speckled,

crackling in its blue depths—
into their old icebox waiting

all winter for something to protect.
Stuffing kindling into the cast-

iron stove. Scrambling eggs,
boiling their last water—

so next morning carrying jugs
up the mountain. Hopping boulder

to boulder. The depth of his handprint
when he leans into plump moss,

cushion of pine needles where he steps.
Mud trembling where they straddle

the stream, jugs frothing
at the neck as they fill. The boy

watching boulders above for snakes,
the pool below for trout and bass.

Carrying the heavy bottles
back down the slope. At the rusty

outdoor sink, pouring icy,
lambent water over his arms,

down his chest.
All the snowcaps melting.

The Fire

The thrill of simply being
in that place, weekend after weekend,
summer after summer.

He had a father there,
hefting bags, pouring cement,
troweling the patio smooth, a father
who pressed the boy's palms
deep into the drying stoop,
carved his name beneath.

He had a mother
bathing him each evening
in a big metal tub,
slowly washing his back
in firelight. They'd laugh at a joke
he can never remember, or she'd ask
about his day. He wants to report

how much he loved that cabin, that pool, his body
stretched full-length on the forest
floor, ladybugs swarming his arms;

loved the glass-eyed moose
over the couch, horseshoes arcing
high in the noon sun;
loved that woman who suddenly left,
that man whose fury and despair
made him burn it all down.

He wants to tell them both
he felt each pine cone
pop, each log explode, each
letter of his name contort
beyond recognition—

Helpless as the icebox
protecting nothing,
he saw the patio, the fireplace,
the moosehead, rats' nests, all
the varnished rafters, the chimney,
flagpole and gate, the forest
as far as the eye can see
(he wasn't there, but he saw),
tree by tree, going up in flames,
then Capricorn, Water Jug, Coffin Corner....

The Ashes

Arms heavy with lunchbox and books,
he's walking in a city far away,
in the ebb and flow of fog,
past spindly ginkgoes, stucco houses.

He's okay in fog. He can't feel
his footsteps against cracked sidewalks,
only the different depths
silence brings, the sensation of falling

light as a pine needle onto a path.
Quiet as a stream under leaves,
he drifts all morning past porches,
shrubs and lawns. No sky. No glyphs.

That oak the charred axis
of a failed universe.
Still he clings to his rope
knotted to nothing, swinging up

in memory, toward Water Jug,
Icebox, Nippenowausee,
toward Ladybug, Horseshoe, Moosehead,
Mother and Father. He's ready now,

whenever I need him, to plummet, arms wide,
down into that smoldering ashen world,
down with boyhood's tenacious hunger,
down to where it all realigns again.

IV

Demolition

Facing my childhood home,
I see clothes piled on the porch, the screen door
hanging from a hinge. No souvenir plates
in the dining room, I'm sure, the cuckoo clock
an imposing absence. The want that built you
left you behind. Oh, House,

once dazzling in sunlight,
now a ghost unheeded. No one else recalls
the way you held against our storms,
our shifting dreams. Perhaps you wove them,
room to room, with light and shadow
and barely audible breathing.

You flew at times,
and I on crest of roof sailed with you
above the esplanade. I heard you weep some nights,
but why, with walls so thick and sure?
But, yes, your plaster peeled,
and, yes, wind blistered
doorways and sills.

Home from school,
I knew your smile as we played: a creak,
a slam, a thump or moan, and I'd
race upstairs or down. And now
what game of pretend could save you:
sleek ship borne on waves of heat,
the pines tall breakers above you?

Or is Fresno in August Troy on fire
and I'm Aeneas ready to hoist you

to my shoulders, carry you
through the flames? Let's go back

beyond the truth, to where your front porch is always
freshly painted green and crawlway vents call out
your bright future. Let's not imagine
the wrecking ball's impending arc.
Bulldozers scraping away your foundation.
Silence hovering with clouds of dust
before the space you were

gets filled with someone else's dream.

Adolescence

Summer mornings, air shimmered
    as the sun climbed the Sierras.
Dirt clods released what little
    moisture they had. The pomegranate
outside my window

held as heat waves rose. Afternoons,
    the drone of swamp-coolers yard to yard
as I walked to the Fresno High pool—
    rows of bodies fun to step on
when the lifeguard wasn't looking,

then bolting into the deep end
    with a huge splash; sting of chlorine
as I watched from the bottom,
    torsos, legs and arms
bobbing, a face

plunging toward me.

↯

Who dared me
    to go off the high dive?
I climbed the dripping ladder
    slowly, looked down at the melting
parking lot, the city wrapped in haze,

felt the dip and heft
    of the trembling board. My knees
locked, stomach wrenched—
    like when Arlene, my cousin,
with a strange look

raised her skirt to show me
    her new panties—
I backed up,
    covered my eyes
and let the tears come.

↙

It took me all of high school
    to coax some girl
into the back seat of my old
    Dodge, one cramped position
after another on the squeaky,

unraveling Naugahyde, my hands groping
    under tight clothes for moist skin,
hardening nipples, bodies gone
    to the motion of hips. *No,*
she pushed, pulled away. *I can't.*

Why not?
    Why? Hot breath
fogging the windows.
    Lighting cigarettes.
Slowly sinking back down....

↙

Entering her was like stepping
    into shimmering air
when I finally went off the high dive,
    rode waves of heat to the clear
blue below. Body smack

opened the surface. Plunging deeper,
    deeper, till our bodies rose

of their own weight, our breath
    not quite air, not quite
water. Groping to find each other's

clothes, a sock missing,
    panties crumpled
on the floorboard. Night's heat
    going nowhere. I drove her home
at dawn, parked a block

from her house.
    Leaning to strap her shoe
established the distance.
    A quick kiss, then gone.
That mingling gone. That new

pleasure that wouldn't let me be.
    I drove the long way home,
climbed the rattling trellis, pulled myself
    though the window and fell
to my bed. When I woke

the pomegranate was gone.

Good Posture

An infant lowered into this body,
expected to find it compatible
—how to adjust to strange flesh?
Hold it stiff as a statue, eyes
milk-white in prayer, so Sister
Cordelia taught us. At seventy she tottered
to her room in the far corner
of the dormitory, past fifty adolescent boys
drifting in desire. Told never
to touch ourselves under the covers,
we could see through windows painted white
her diffuse shadow undressing,
our bodies filling with a grace of sorts
till spasms of guilt fixed the great distance
between heaven and boys.

                        Sundays
the litany of mouths would open for the wafer:
bad to chew it, bad to swallow it,
good to savor that body melting
on our tongues. Shoulder to shoulder, we knelt
and stood, sang hymns to a Christ
with nailed palms, straight back,
while our own hands smelled of rosewater,
our neatly combed heads like fresh
petals the nuns constantly eyed

—sternly if we leaned forward or backward
or turned toward the girls' pews
meant to be beyond imagination.
Marching single-file to class or chapel
and back, sitting at long silent tables

for meals, rows of coats on hooks
with our numbers above our heads, shoes
and galoshes in crowded cubbyholes
—we lived our mackerel days
like our nights, hands folded,
mouths closed, backs straight....

That day I stole everyone's pencils
during recess, how was I to know
stealing was worse than poor posture?
I stood erect as Sister Leonardo
tipped my desk to a shower of #2
Ticonderogas. Hands punished,
I learned to answer with a *maxima culpa*,
then retreated to the fields to soothe my aching palms
in muddy grass, slumped there with snails
struggling over the fluting of rotting leaves
toward a different heaven.

I never wanted this flesh
nor this particular view. Better a salmon
swimming against the years,
mouth gaping, body stiffening
with these others bumping against me.
The riddle of posture solved
at last, we'd leap and leap
till we'd left our rigid bodies
on a milky shore, pure spirits
entering a heaven
    dark as the habits
        of the Sisters of Mercy.

Maybe, CA

When I arrived, your gaze was wandering
beyond the tangle of tubes and blinking lights,
beyond the weary, anxious looks
of the son and daughter you raised,
searching the endless white of the ceiling.
For what? A nurse poked your foot with a needle
to show me you couldn't respond, only the dull
rhythm of chin squeezing to neck
and back, as if swimming against the current—
of what stream? Face wedged between sheets.
The grey hair you pampered
sheared off for the surgery you wouldn't
wake from, those tiny clots
huge boulders blocking your veins,
slowing, I imagined, the vague pulsing
across your forehead that, yes,
was my forehead too. Same cheekbones.
Same eyes. I wanted to grab your bony shoulders,
pull you to me and shout—*Who
are you?* Two days later
I knew: you were ash in a bag.

↓

When we emptied your trailer,
my sister took the lamp in the corner,
my brother your 78s, and I
the photos you thumbed those long
nights of pain coursing your body:

You and three men, what memory?
You and two women, whose party?
You with a low neckline, dancing alone?

Uncle Duke on a porch
with what's his name, your first
husband, the one who took you from that Sierra mill town
to work the clubs and restaurants
in Reno.

You told me once (just once)
that the months you carried me inside you
were your only time of peace there. For years
I imagined you in your yellow waitress uniform
walking the Truckee River, stopping at the bridge
over the small set of falls, the leaves
on the oaks a deeper yellow,
almost ready to fall.

↯

Your will made it clear.
No name carved in marble
for you. No preacher or coffin.
Just ashes scattered in the place you were born.
When we arrived your home wasn't there.
Nothing left of the mill where your father worked
sometimes. No scattered wooden shacks
they called a town back then. Just a collapsing
train trestle, a mud-caked road
rutted by four-wheel-drives. The town had moved
a mile closer to Reno, accepted
its indefiniteness by taking a new name—
Maybe, CA, the sign on the highway read.
And so you returned
with two sisters, three brothers,
the son and daughter you raised
and the son you didn't,

each tossing a handful of you
into the clear mountain air.

↙

The fistful I tossed
took the shape of a mask.
The eyes two dark spaces
hovering, staring back.
The mouth about to speak....

But at last you settled,
keeping your secrets, as always,
to yourself, coming to rest
where my brother propped your favorite picture,
a younger you, hair in tight curls,
three rows of pearls around your neck.

But some of you drifted to the cleft of a pine.
Some wedged in the boulders by the stream.
Some mingled with the dust on our cars.
And some fell back to us.

↙

Now, as I fly over the ocean,
a veil of clouds below, the taste of ash
still on my tongue, a thin grinding
between molars, the few flakes I secreted away
deep in my luggage, you are, as always,
intensely vague in my thoughts, but calm now,
drifting the shallows of an all-white stream
I've imagined for you, the steady hiss
of the falls, the eddies like your craving to be alone
churning against my craving
for your warm breath, light chafing

of your chin on my cheek. Not the fixed weight
of your absence, this knot of perplexity
you left deep in my heart.
Was it fear or wisdom that made you
never fight to regain me?
Your box of snapshots what explained
it all away? The image that comes to mind—

a woman with a face of ash
saying she lived her life, raised
a son and daughter, safe in her distance.
Those words, like forgiveness, its possibility,
remain behind a veil of pines and a sign
for Maybe, CA.

Acknowledgments

The author would like to thank the editors of the following journals which originally published poems appearing in this collection, some in earlier versions:

Arts & Letters: "Constellations"
Calliope: "Maybe, CA," "Good Posture," "The Trouble with Gender"
Georgetown Review: "Chosen"
Lips: "Adolescence," "Dutch Clock," "Rummaging," "Ars Poetica"
New Works Review: "After the Divorce," "That Blur," "A Child's 99,"
    "Devotion," "Driving Thessaly," "Good Posture,"
Nimrod International Journal: "About the Bears"
Oberon: "Demolition," "The Immortals"
Paterson Literary Review: "Chosen," "Divorce"
Southern Poetry Review: "Before Kodachrome"
St. Petersburg Review: "Days of August"
Suisun Valley Review: "2619 Van Ness Blvd"
Valparaiso Quarterly Review: "First Journey, Alone"
Waywiser Press: "Keeping the Monsters Moving," "New Parents"

Special thanks is also due to the Poetry Center of Passaic County Community College for awarding "Chosen" the Allen Ginsberg Poetry Award and "Divorce" an Editor's Choice Award.

Cover art: "Eye" by Iva Villi; photo of the author by Litsa Papalexiou; cover and book design by Diane Kistner (dkistner@futurecycle.org); typeface, Chapparal Pro

About FutureCycle Press

FutureCycle Press is dedicated to publishing lasting English-language poetry and flash fiction books, chapbooks, and anthologies in both print-on-demand and ebook formats. Founded in 2007 by long-time independent editor/publishers and partners Diane Kistner and Robert S. King, the press incorporated as a nonprofit in 2012. A number of our editors are distinguished poets and authors in their own right, and we have been actively involved in the small press movement going back to the early seventies. Nobody gets paid. We do what we do for love.

Our annual anthology, *FutureCycle*, combines poetry and flash fiction. The FutureCycle Poetry Book Prize and honorarium is awarded annually for the best full-length volume of poetry we publish in a calendar year. We are dedicated to giving all authors we publish the care their work deserves, making our catalog of titles the most distinguished it can be, and paying forward any earnings to fund more great books.

We've learned a few things about independent publishing over the years. We've also evolved a unique, resilient publishing model that allows us to focus mainly on vetting and preserving for posterity the most books of exceptional quality without becoming overwhelmed with bookkeeping and mailing, fundraising activities, or taxing editorial and production "bubbles." To find out more about what we are doing, come see us at www.futurecycle.org.

www.ingramcontent.com/pod-product-compliance
Lightning Source LLC
LaVergne TN
LVHW020938090426
835512LV00020B/3417